PHOTOBOOK
Willie
COPYRIGHT ©2022 BY KDP 01

Willie

6.5
Z·99

TS ESP 746
TS ESP 746

mola
mola

BA 64

НАДЕЖДА
ВЛАДИВОСТОК

EAGLE
De CHAN

BESSIE

Willie

AYC
25

@Stralsundpassion

1277

EUROPA

PICTON CASTLE

IRISH OFFSHORE SAILING

GBR
1388N

Printed in Great Britain
by Amazon

11656729R00025